Let's Play Dress Up

I WANT TO BE A KNIGHT

Rebekah Joy Shirley
Photography by Chris Fairclough

WINDMILL
BOOKS

New York

Published in 2012 by Windmill Books, An Imprint of Rosen Publishing
29 East 21st Street, New York, NY 10010

Series concept: Discovery Books Ltd, 2 College Street, Ludlow, Shropshire SY8 1AN, UK
www.discoverybooks.net

Managing editor: Laura Durman
Editor: Rebecca Hunter
Designer: Blink Media
Photography: Chris Fairclough

Library of Congress Cataloging-in-Publication Data

Shirley, Rebekah Joy.
 I want to be a knight / by Rebekah Joy Shirley. — 1st ed.
    p. cm. — (Let's play dress up)
 Includes index.
 ISBN 978-1-61533-354-7 (library binding) — ISBN 978-1-61533-392-9 (pbk.) — ISBN 978-1-61533-457-5 (6-pack)
 1. Handicraft—Juvenile literature. 2. Children's costumes—Juvenile literature. 3. Knights and knighthood—Juvenile literature. 4. Armor, Medieval—Juvenile literature. I. Title.
 TT160.S394 2012
 646.4'78—dc22
                                   2010050406

The author and photographer would like to acknowledge the following for their help in preparing this book: the staff and pupils of Chad Vale Primary School, Cyrus Dhariwal, Rory Munro, Zaydan Law, Abbie Sangha, Oliver Town, Lydia Wright.

Printed in China

CPSIA Compliance Information: Batch #AS2011WM: For Further Information contact Windmill Books, New York, New York at 1-866-478-0556
SL001741US

CONTENTS

Some of the projects in this book may require the use of needles, pins, and safety pins. We would advise that young children are supervised by a responsible adult.

KEEP YOUR HEAD!

Making a costume can be messy work! Make sure you cover all surfaces with newspaper before you start.

Knights often fought on the battlefield. They had to protect themselves from **enemies**. Knights needed helmets to protect their heads.

Make a helmet using:
A balloon
A tape measure
Newspaper, torn into strips
Craft glue and a paintbrush
Silver paint and a paintbrush
Silver sequins
Silver fabric
An old cereal box
A pair of scissors
A ruler

TIP:
If you want to make the glue runnier, mix four teaspoons of water with two tablespoons of glue in a jar.

1 Measure around your head with a tape measure. Blow up a balloon so that it is slightly bigger than your head measurement. Cover the top half of the balloon in three layers of newspaper and glue.

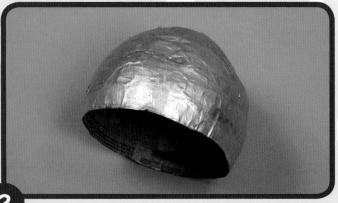

2 When the glue is dry, pop the balloon. Trim the edges of the dome and paint it silver.

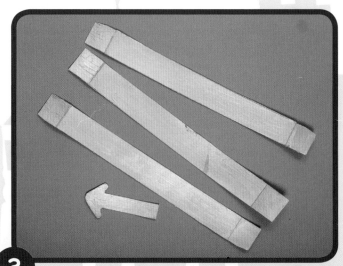

3 Cut three long strips of cardboard (12 in. x 2 in.) from a cereal packet. Cut an arrow-shaped nose guard from the cardboard, too. Paint all the pieces silver.

4

TIP:
Use clothespins to hold everything in place while the glue dries.

4 Glue two of the strips around the bottom of your helmet and one over the top. Trim off any left-over bits. Glue the nose guard in the middle where all three strips meet.

5 Stick silver sequins along the strips of cardboard.

6 Cut a rectangle of silver fabric about 8 in. x 12 in. Glue one long edge inside the back of the helmet to make a neck guard.

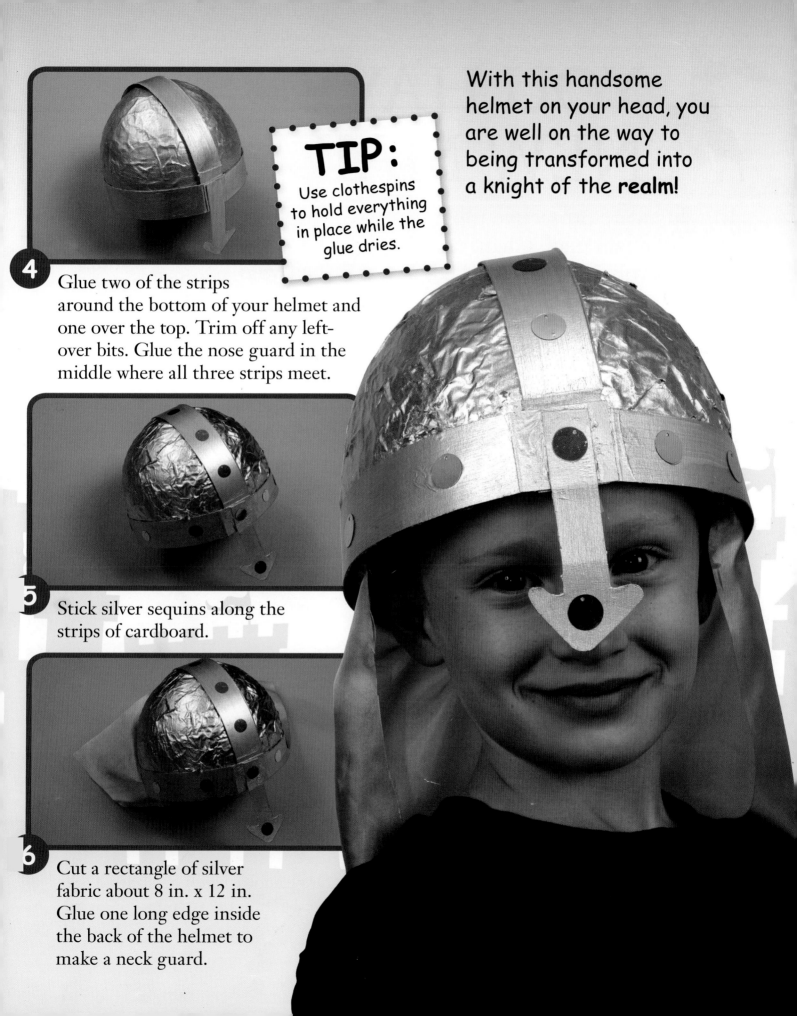

YOU HAVE NEW MAIL

Knights wore protective tops made of chain mail. Chain mail is made from iron rings linked together in rows.

To make your own chain mail vest you will need:
A gray long-sleeved T-shirt
A black permanent marker pen
A large plastic bottle top

1 Draw around the bottle top in black marker pen to make a curved row of circles on the T-shirt.

TIP:

Put two sheets of newspaper inside your T-shirt to stop the marker pen leaking through to the other side.

2 Draw another row of circles overlapping the first.

6

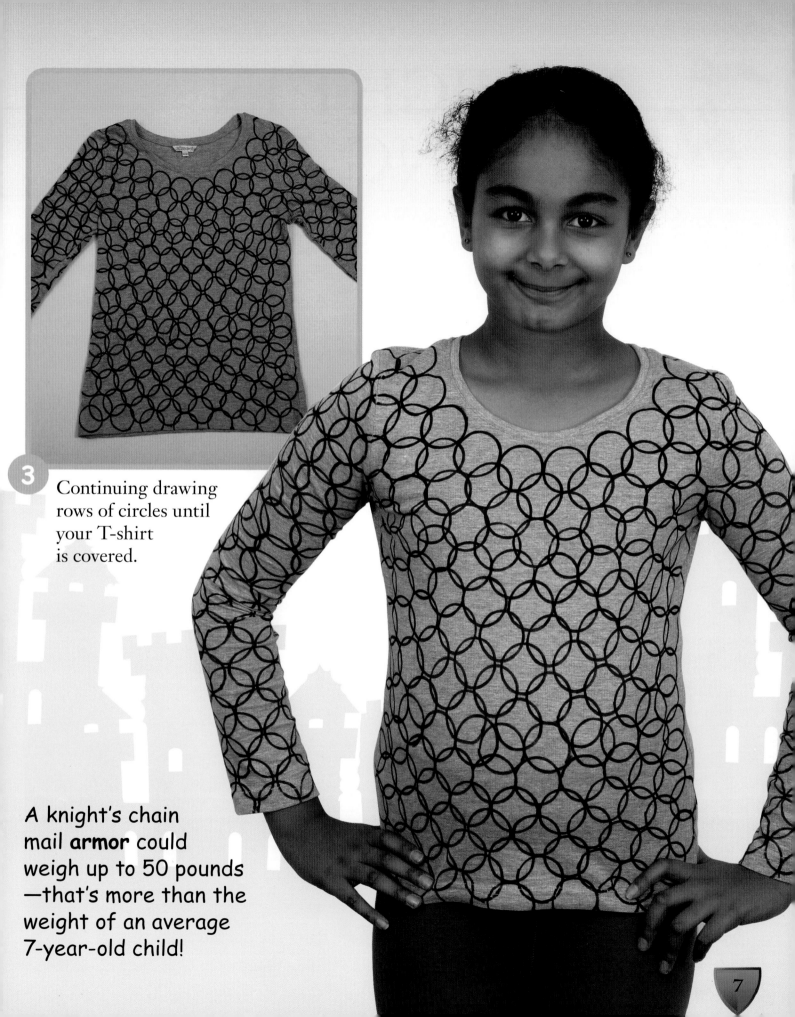

3 Continuing drawing rows of circles until your T-shirt is covered.

A knight's chain mail **armor** could weigh up to 50 pounds —that's more than the weight of an average 7-year-old child!

A KNIGHT IN SHINING ARMOR

A knight's arms, legs, shoulders, elbows, and knees were protected by large pieces of metal called plate armor.

1 Ask an adult to cut the tops and bottoms off four plastic bottles to make plastic tubes.

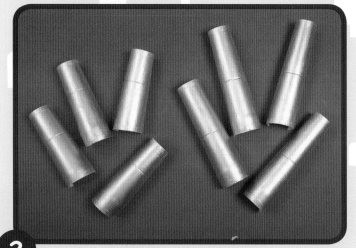

2 Cut the tubes in half lengthwise and paint them silver.

3 Paint the dust masks silver.

8

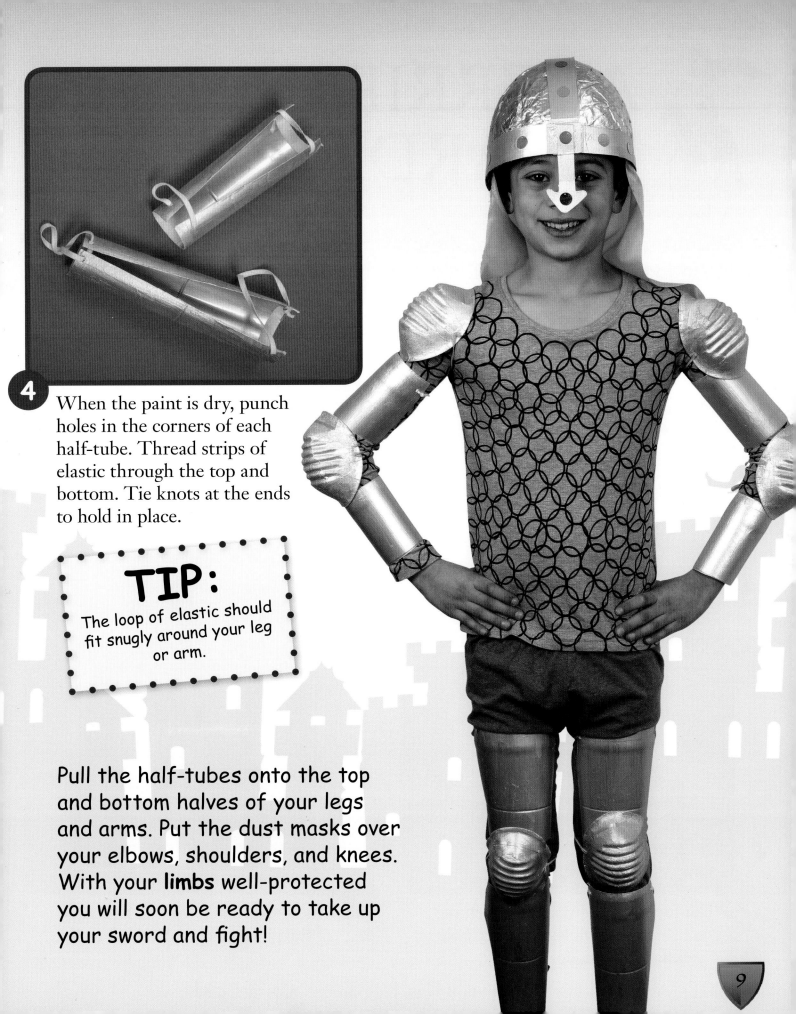

4 When the paint is dry, punch holes in the corners of each half-tube. Thread strips of elastic through the top and bottom. Tie knots at the ends to hold in place.

TIP:
The loop of elastic should fit snugly around your leg or arm.

Pull the half-tubes onto the top and bottom halves of your legs and arms. Put the dust masks over your elbows, shoulders, and knees. With your **limbs** well-protected you will soon be ready to take up your sword and fight!

A TERRIFIC TABARD

A knight wore another piece of clothing over the top of their chain mail, called a tabard. The tabard often had a symbol on the front.

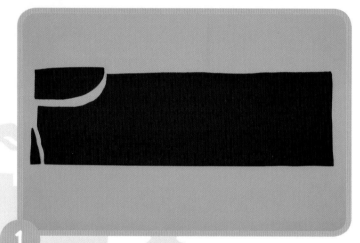

1 Fold a pillowcase in half. Cut the corners off the closed end of the pillowcase as shown in the picture.

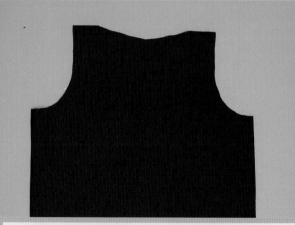

2 Unfold the pillowcase to check the size of the armholes and neck hole you have just made.

3 Glue gold ribbon around the edges of the pillowcase to make a **border**.

10

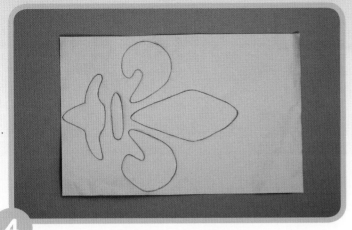

4 Draw a symbol onto the back of the gold paper. The symbol could be a cross, a flower, or an animal, such as a lion.

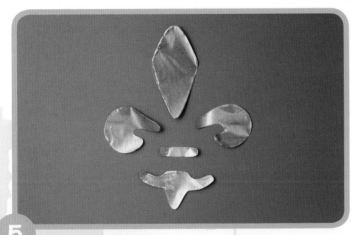

5 Cut the shape out.

6 Glue the shape onto the front of the pillowcase.

Now you are looking the part, and fit for a place at the king's court!

11

GAUNTLET GLOVES

Knights wore gloves called gauntlets to protect their hands and arms in battle. Gauntlets sometimes had spikes on the wrists to make them look **fearsome**.

To make your gauntlets you will need:
- Thin cardboard
- A pair of scissors
- Black paint and a paintbrush
- A silver pen
- Craft glue and a paintbrush
- A pen or pencil
- A ruler
- A pair of black gloves

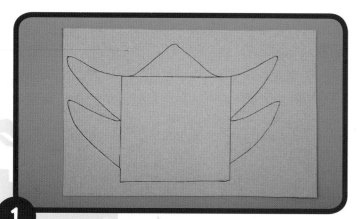

1 Draw a square slightly wider than your wrist onto cardboard (about 4 in. x 4 in.). Draw spikes coming out from the sides of the square and a triangle at one end.

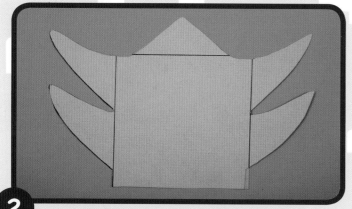

2 Cut the shape out. Use this shape as a template to cut out three more cardboard shapes.

3 Paint all four shapes black.

4 Decorate two of the shapes using a silver pen.

5 Glue the edges of each plain shape to a decorated shape.

Put on your gloves and slip the cardboard shapes over the top. With these gauntlets, you are ready for a **bout** of **jousting!**

A TRUSTY SWORD

Knights carried sharp, shiny swords which they used to battle with monsters.

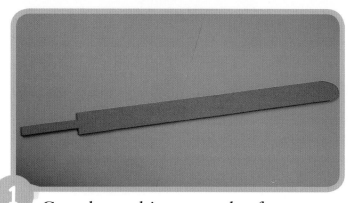

1 Cut a long, thin rectangle of cardboard that is 24 in. long and 3 in. wide. Cut a narrow section at the bottom of the blade to make the handle. It should be the width of the cardboard tube and about 6 in. long.

TIP: Make sure your blade has a rounded end. Otherwise it could be dangerous!

2 Cut two pointed pieces of cardboard the same width as the tube and 12 in. long. Glue them to the handle to strengthen it. Paint the blade silver.

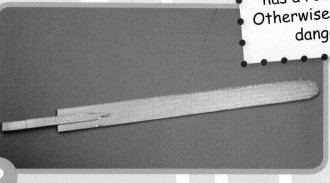

3 Paint the cardboard tube gold and glue a plastic bottle top onto the end.

14

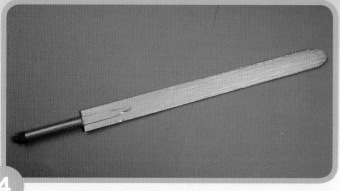

4 Push the tube onto the narrow part of the blade and glue it in place.

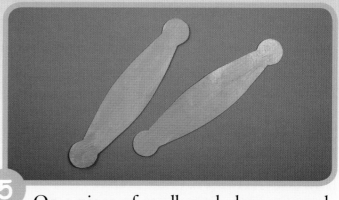

5 On a piece of cardboard, draw an oval 7 in. long and 2 in. high. Then draw around a bottle top at each end of the oval. Copy this shape and cut them both out. Paint both shapes gold.

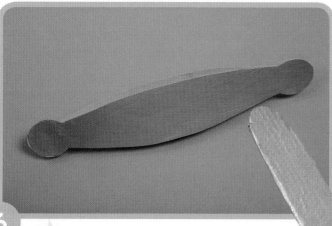

Now you are ready to take on a dragon!

6 Glue the circles at the end of the shapes together to make the **hilt**.

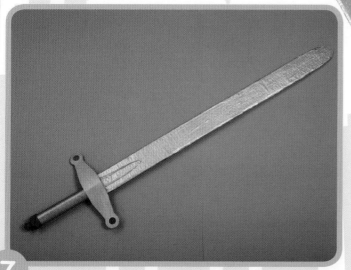

7 Push the hilt over the tube and glue in place where the handle meets the blade. Glue sequins onto each side of the hilt.

A DEFENSIVE SHIELD

Knights used a shield to protect themselves from their enemies' swords.

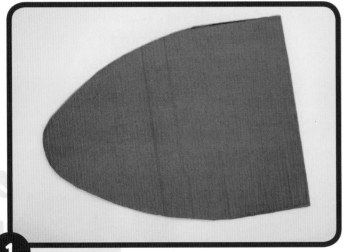

1 Draw a shield shape onto cardboard and cut it out.

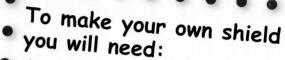

To make your own shield you will need:
- A piece of cardboard (16 in. wide and 20 in. long)
- String
- Silver paint and a paintbrush
- Gold paint and a paintbrush
- Craft glue and a paintbrush
- A pair of scissors
- Thin cardboard
- A ruler

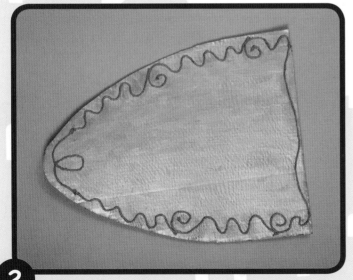

2 Paint the shield silver and the string gold. When the paint is dry, glue the string in a pattern around the edge of the shield.

3 Cut a rectangle out of thin cardboard that is around 10 in. long and 7 in. wide. Fold a strip that is half an inch wide along both of the shorter edges.

4 Glue the folded strips to the back of the shield, making a loop big enough to fit your arm through. This will allow you to hold the shield.

Knights often decorated their shield with a **coat of arms**. Find out how to do this next.

FAMILY PRIDE

A knight's shield bore a design called a coat of arms. This gave information about the history of the family.

To make your own coat of arms you will need:
- Paper
- Cardboard
- A pair of scissors
- Colored paints and a paintbrush
- A pen or pencil
- Craft glue and a paintbrush

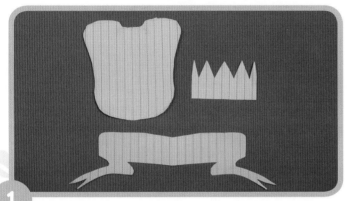

1 Fold a piece of paper in half and draw half a shield shape, a crown, and a scroll. Cut them out and unfold the paper. Your shapes will be **symmetrical.**

2 Draw a lion shape on paper and cut it out.

3 Draw around all of the paper shapes on cardboard and cut them out. Draw and cut out two lions.

4 Draw a cross in the middle of the small shield to divide it into four sections. Paint the sections different colors.

You can find out if your family has a coat of arms on the Internet. If it does you could draw your own coat of arms and put it on your shield.

5 Paint all of the other shapes, too.

6 Glue all of the shapes in the center of your shield.

19

A LANCE FOR LIFE

Knights used to **compete** in jousting games. They charged at each other with a **lance** and tried to knock each other off their horses.

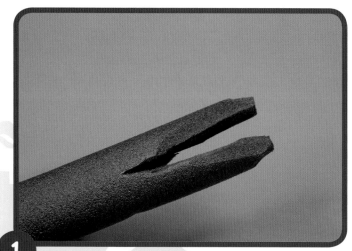

1 Cut a long, thin triangle out of one end of the foam pipe.

TIP: You could use a small plate to draw around.

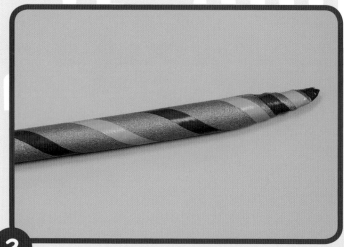

2 Stick colored tape around the pipe at an angle. Use the tape to shape the cut end into a point.

3 Draw a circle onto cardboard and cut it out. The circle should have a diameter of about 6 in. Cut out a smaller circle the same size as the pipe.

What do you call a knight that can't stop fighting?
Sir Lance-a-lot!

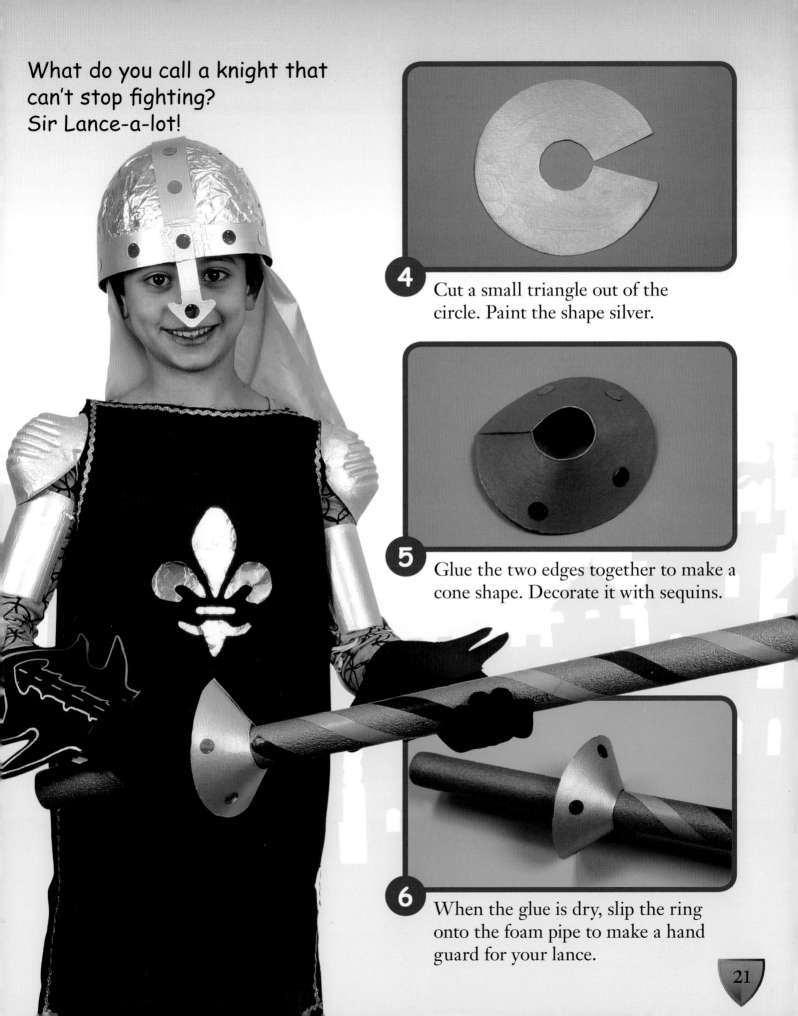

4 Cut a small triangle out of the circle. Paint the shape silver.

5 Glue the two edges together to make a cone shape. Decorate it with sequins.

6 When the glue is dry, slip the ring onto the foam pipe to make a hand guard for your lance.

FLY THE FLAG

Knights often carried flags into battle. The colors of their flag showed which side they were fighting for.

Make your own flag using:
Dowel pole (about 3 ft. long)
Colored tape
Gold ribbon
A Styrofoam ball
Gold paint and a paintbrush
Two different-colored lengths of material (each about 30 in. long)
Craft glue and a paintbrush
A pair of scissors

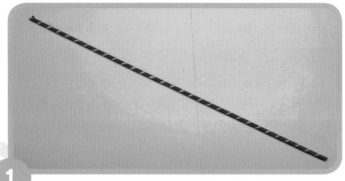

1 Twist colored tape around the dowel pole.

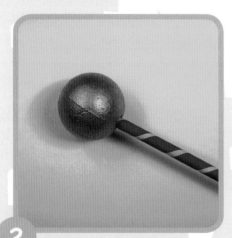

2 Paint the Styrofoam ball gold. Then ask an adult to help you to push it onto the end of the pole.

3 Cut a long triangle out of each length of material. Position the triangles so that one overlaps the other slightly at the widest point and glue them together.

4 Place glue around the edges of the triangles and fold them over.

5 Make a tunnel for the flagpole by folding the side edge over by 1 in. Glue it in place.

6 Turn the material over and glue gold ribbon around the edges of the triangles.

7 Guide the dowel pole through the material tunnel.

Wave your flag proudly as you head off to fight for your king and country.

23

GLOSSARY

armor (AR-mer) metal clothing worn for protection
border (BOR-der) a strip or pattern around the edge of something
bout (BOWT) a short fight or competition
coat of arms (KOHT UV AHRMZ) the design on a shield that is linked to a particular family
compete (kum-PEET) to take part in a competition or game
fearsome (FIR-sum) very frightening
hilt (HILT) the handle of a sword or dagger
jousting (JOWST-ing) fighting between knights on horseback, using lances
lance (LANTS) a long spear used by knights
limbs (LIMZ) arms or legs
realm (RELM) a country ruled by a king or queen
symmetrical (sih-MEH-trih-kul) being exactly the same on both sides

FURTHER INFORMATION

MacDonald, Fiona. *How to Be a Medieval Knight*. Washington, DC: National Geographic Children's Books, 2007.

MacDonald, Fiona. *You Wouldn't Want to Be a Medieval Knight*. Danbury, CT: Children's Press, 2004.

Morris, Gerald. *The Adventures of Sir Gawain the True*. Boston, MA: Houghton Mifflin Harcourt, 2011.

WEB SITES

For Web resources related to the subject of this book, go to: www.windmillbooks.com/weblinks and select this book's title.

INDEX